Reycraft Books
55 Fifth Avenue
New York, NY 10003

Reycraftbooks.com

Reycraft Books is a trade imprint and trademark of Newmark Learning, LLC.

This edition is published by arrangement with Hsiao Lu Publishing Co., Ltd. © Hsiao Lu Publishing Co., Ltd.

Library of Congress Control Number: 2020900898

ISBN: 978-1-4788-6954-2

Printed in Dongguan, China. 8557/1020/17446

10 9 8 7 6 5 4 3 2

First Edition Hardcover published by Reycraft Books 2020

Reycraft Books and Newmark Learning, LLC, support diversity and the First Amendment, and celebrate the right to read.

Woodpecker Girl

written by Chingyen Liu
and I-Tsun Chiang
Illustrated by Heidi Doll

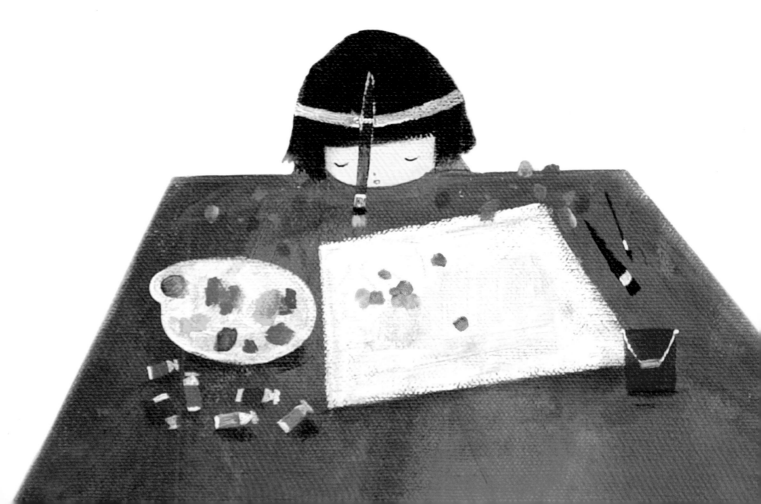

I am a woodpecker who loves to draw.

But I can't hop on branches or fly
freely in the sky like a real woodpecker.

My brain lacked oxygen when I was born.

From that moment on, my body and my brain have worked against each other.

When I want to greet someone, my neck swerves back.

When I want to talk, I can only make "ee-ee-ah-ah" sounds.

When I want to smile, my face looks angry.

I had to start school sooner than other children.

I needed to learn how to keep my body in balance and control the turning of my neck.

I use my hands and feet to feel the shape and temperature of things. I am just learning how to talk.

These things might be a piece of cake for most people, but for me they are very difficult.

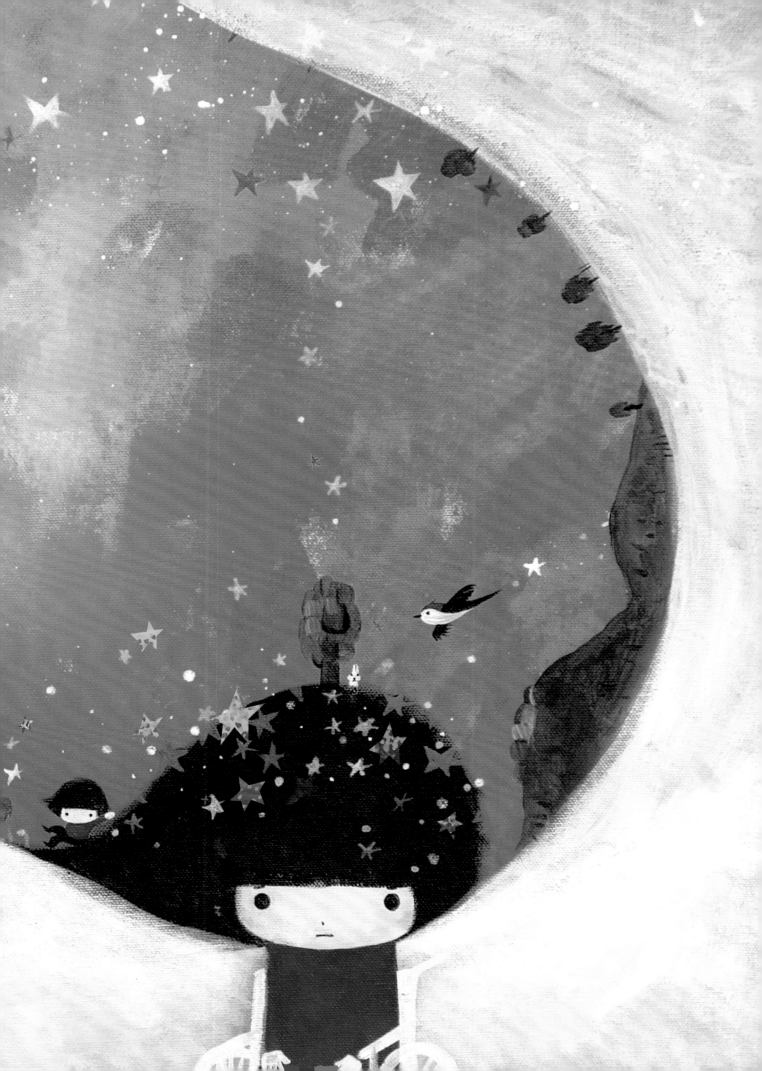

You might wonder how it feels to see other children jumping and playing when I can only stay in one place.

I hear people sing. If I could sing, would it be beautiful?

All I can do is sit quietly.

My little sister chases and plays with our puppy, Coco, all day. They have such fun together. But I feel sad.

I want to play with Coco, too. But my wheelchair might roll onto him.

Coco loves to put his paws on my knees. I know he wants to cuddle with me, but I can't.

I try to accept the way that I am.

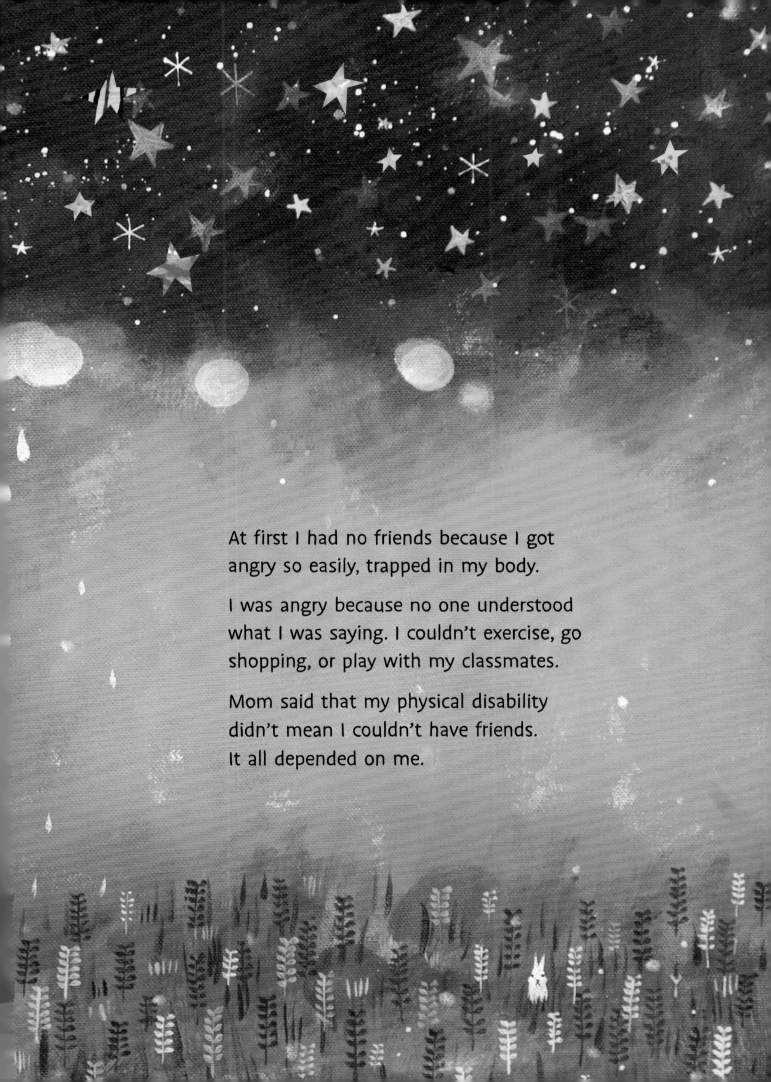

At first I had no friends because I got angry so easily, trapped in my body.

I was angry because no one understood what I was saying. I couldn't exercise, go shopping, or play with my classmates.

Mom said that my physical disability didn't mean I couldn't have friends. It all depended on me.

Mom was right. So, I tried to change.
I started talking with my classmates,
using a computer.

Now I have some friends. One of my
friends is like a big sister to me.

She can do so much. She can play the piano. She can sing. She can bake, too.

She says that one day she will open a bakery filled with music. It will bring happiness to all of her customers.

Can I bring happiness to other people, too? I wonder. What can I do?

Dad says that I can paint.

But how can a girl who can't even hold
a pencil paint?

How is it possible?

My art teacher smiles at me and says,
"No problem. I'll figure out a way."

The first time I wore the headband with
a brush attached, my classmates laughed.
They said I looked like a woodpecker.

I did look weird.

However, my teacher was proud of his invention.

He put on the headband and showed me how to paint with it.

The headband felt uncomfortable. It made it difficult to control the brush.

I had to keep nodding dot-by-dot to paint the picture I saw in my mind. I admit, I did look like a woodpecker.

It was exhausting painting this way. But once I put on the headband, I felt like I was spreading my wings and flying freely in the sky.

I wake up at dawn to the rooster crowing, loudly and clearly.

I see the sun rising. The bright and warm light fills me with hope.

I follow behind the girls strolling happily in the forest. I eavesdrop on them whispering secrets.

I fly over a pond with blooming water lilies
and see the fish playfully swimming.

I fly over the meadow covered with colorful wildflowers and play hide-and-seek with the clouds.

I listen to the waves lapping against the shore. Sometimes gentle. Sometimes rough.

I follow the shining stars and fly home in the starry
night, softly saying goodnight to the yellow kitten
sleeping on the wall.

I love painting. I don't mind that the way I paint is different from others.

I love painting. I don't mind painting dot-by-dot, slowly, even when it makes my neck so sore.

I love painting. So, I will bear it because . . .

I am going to be a woodpecker that brings happiness to everyone.

2011/Rooster

2008/Fish

2009/Stroll in the Park

2011/Lotus

2008/Dawning Light

2013/In Starry Night

2012/Under the Sky

2009/Waves

2009/Sunrise with Hope

2010/Contentment

Author
Chingyen Liu

 Chingyen Liu writes children's books and hosts radio and TV shows. He has been telling stories to children for more than thirty years. He is also a two-time winner of the Golden Bell Award in Taiwan for the best children's TV show host.

When he first met Yipei, the girl on whom *Woodpecker Girl* is based, he was amazed at her talent and her drive to overcome her physical limitations. He spent time talking to her about her difficulties and her painting process. Despite all her challenges and how misunderstood she felt, once she discussed the pleasure painting brought her it was as if she were a glorious woodpecker flying freely through the forest. It was as if she were no longer trapped inside her body. Their discussions and his observations of her painting helped him decide how to write and structure the book.

Chingyen Liu worked closely with I-Tsun Chiang, a professor of special education at National Taiwan Normal University and an expert on children with disabilities, to review and edit the story. Both wanted every child, physically challenged or not, to understand the strength needed to face life's obstacles and to see Yipei's story as an example of what is possible.

Author
I-Tsun Chiang

I-Tsun Chiang is a professor of special education at National Taiwan Normal University. He worked with Chingyen Liu to review and edit *Woodpecker Girl*. His service work and academic research are focused on helping people who face serious physical challenges, including those who have cerebral palsy, like Yipei, the main character.

Cerebral palsy is not contagious. It is a multihandicap that includes problems with movement that develop during childbirth or shortly thereafter. The cause is unknown, but most believe it may result from premature birth, certain infections during pregnancy, exposure to mercury during pregnancy, a difficult delivery where the baby doesn't get enough oxygen, or illnesses after birth, such as meningitis. Cerebral palsy causes damage to the part of the brain that controls body movements and coordination. It can also cause issues with communication, eyesight, hearing, learning, and controlling emotions.

As a result, many are misled into thinking that children with cerebral palsy are less capable. This is not true. Most of these children have the same learning potential as all children. Mr. Chiang believes the world needs to see the talents and potential of people with physical limitations. This is why this book is so important to him.

Illustrator
Heidi Doll

Heidi Doll enjoys nature, animals, and long walks, but most importantly painting. She lives by the sea in Hualien, Taiwan, where she wakes to the smell of coffee each morning and whispers to the stars each night. Some of her books include *The Stars Are Gone* and *Twisted Rabbit*.

She was deeply moved by the story of Yipei because she shares the same passion for painting but has none of the physical limitations. The authors and editors of the book suggested she combine some of Yipei's artwork with her own in the book and mimic Yipei's style, including her brighter color choices—which are unlike the warmer, softer colors Doll normally uses. She wanted readers to feel the persistence and courage of Yipei through her art.

She drew a woodpecker on every spread to represent Yipei and to encourage her to soar with her ideas and talents. The rabbit throughout the book represents her as the guardian of Yipei's dreams. She hopes the book glitters like the nighttime stars in the hearts of children all over the world who read it.

Yipei Huang

Yipei, the main character in *Woodpecker Girl*, was born with cerebral palsy, yet despite her limitations everyone who meets her is struck by her optimism and smile. She has never let her disability stand in the way of her drawing and painting. She believes that "an imperfect body can also lead to a perfect life."

A Note from Yipei's Mother

Yipei is such a lucky girl because she is surrounded by family and teachers who love her. She couldn't hold a pencil, so her teachers first taught her to draw using a computer. At that time, she was drawing random lines and applying layers of color.

She truly learned to draw and paint after she finished junior high school. Her vocational teacher at the National Hemei Experimental School, Mr. Chi-hai Tsai, immediately believed in her and accepted her into the art department.

He carefully observed her and realized that what she could control most was her head. That's when he got the idea to create the headset—a headband with a paintbrush attached—for her to use to paint. Everything started from that magical moment. Yipei went from black-and-white paintings to colorful paintings and from simple thick lines to thin lines with delicate dotted images. What my daughter has achieved is beyond our imagination. Yipei could never be the woodpecker painter without Mr. Tsai.

Every time I see Yipei wearing her headset—nodding and nodding and nodding to dot the paper with paints—I worry she will get too tired. But whenever I ask her, "Are you tired now? Do you need to rest?" she always says, "Of course I am tired, but I like painting so much." I think painting brings her both happiness and a sense of achievement. It has broadened her view of life and truly made it colorful.

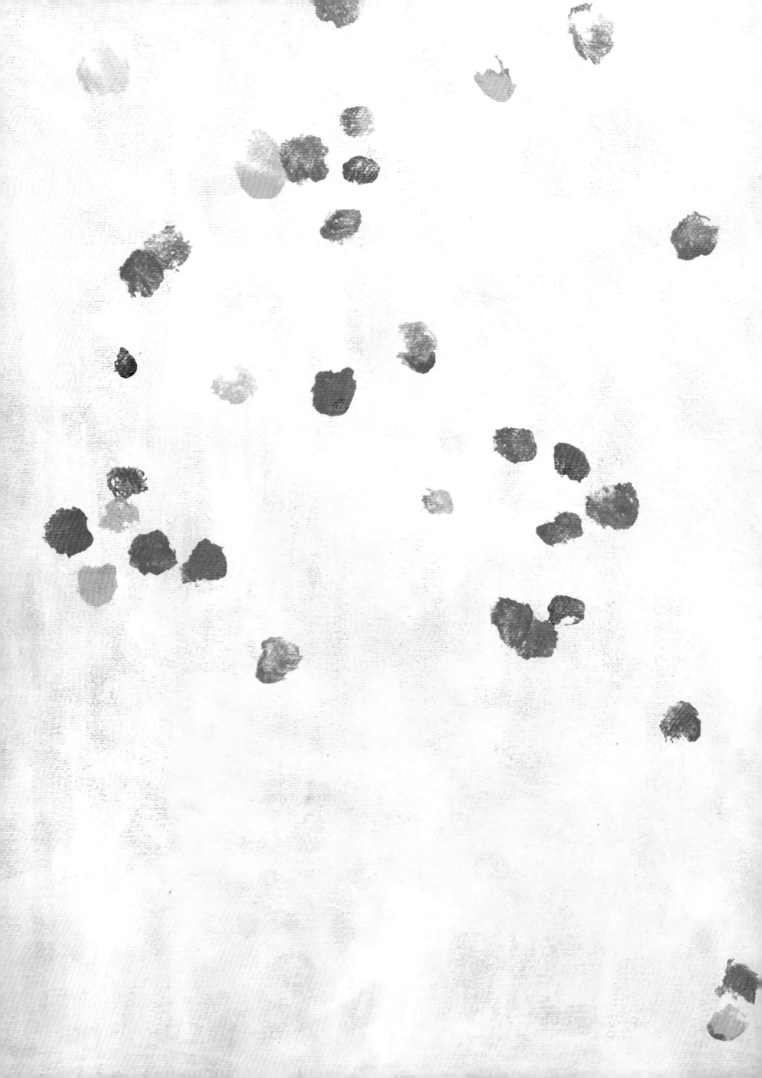